Air Pollution

DISCOVER PICTURES AND FACTS ABOUT AIR POLLUTION FOR KIDS! A CHILDREN'S SCIENCE BOOK

D1608744

Air pollution is another very important fact that you need to understand and keep at. Below you'll learn some important facts about air pollution.

Air pollution actually causes a lot more deaths than you think, and it accounts for about a third of deaths resulting from respiratory diseases, lung cancers, and heart disease.

It has a devastating effect on crops since this can reduce the crop yield. Wheat and soybeans especially are affected by this.

The ozone, along with pollutants from the sunlight also contribute to asthma and chronic respiratory disease.

Almost everyone lives in a place with bad air quality, and if you live near power plants, industrial activity, waste burning, or places with lots of human activity, it'll hurt your health.

Air pollution is made up of biological materials, chemicals, and some particulates, and they're in large amounts.

Air pollution is caused by both humans, and natural contributors, so it isn't just industries, but also forest fires, wind erosion, and volcanic eruptions.

The air pollution actually can also be responsible for a lot of premature deaths every year and is a reason for low birth weight, high blood pressure, and cataracts.

Cities with low and middle-income areas are actually the most affected, and they're subjected to a large amount of unsafe air pollution.

Pregnant woman who live in areas with high traffic has a much higher risk of having children with impaired lung function than those in less polluted areas.

While there are a lot of issues right now, many mayors and town ordinances are taking to reduce it, and if you want to help, you can.

Air pollution is no joke, and it's killing all of us, so you should be informed of why it's happening, and do your part to reduce it.